W9-AZA-351

TURNING POINTS IN US MILITARY HISTORY

THE TET OFFENSIVE

Charlie Samuels

Gareth Stevens
Publishing

Please visit our website, www.garethstevens.com. For a free color catalog of all our high-quality books, call toll-free 1-800-542-2595 or fax 1-877-542-2596.

Library of Congress Cataloging-in-Publication Data

Samuels, Charlie.
The Tet Offensive / by Charlie Samuels.
  p. cm. — (Turning points in US military history)
Includes index.
ISBN 978-1-4824-0436-4 (pbk.)
ISBN 978-1-4824-0438-8 (6-pack)
ISBN 978-1-4824-0435-7 (library binding)
1. Tet Offensive, 1968 — Juvenile literature. 2. Vietnam War, 1961-1975 — Campaigns — Juvenile literature. I. Samuels, Charlie, 1961- II. Title.
DS557.8.T4 S26 2014
959.704—dc23

Published in 2014 by
Gareth Stevens Publishing
111 East 14th Street, Suite 349
New York, NY 10003

For Brown Bear Books Ltd:
Editorial Director: Lindsey Lowe
Managing Editor: Tim Cooke
Children's Publisher: Anne O'Daly
Design Manager: Keith Davis
Designer: Lynne Lennon
Picture Manager: Sophie Mortimer
Production Director: Alastair Gourlay

Picture Credits:
Front Cover: US National Archives

All images US National Archives except:
Robert Hunt Library: 6, 13, 14, 15, 16, 17, 20, 36, 38, 43.

All Artworks © Brown Bear Books Ltd

Brown Bear Books has made every attempt to contact the copyright holder. If you have any information please contact smortimer@brownbearbooks.co.uk

Manufactured in the United States of America

CPSIA compliance information: Batch #CW14GS. For further information contact Gareth Stevens, New York, New York at 1-800-542-2595.

CONTENTS

INTRODUCTION

The Tet Offensive of January 30, 1968, marked the turning point of the Vietnam War. It was a major assault by the North Vietnamese Army and Vietcong guerrillas against US and South Vietnamese positions in cities throughout South Vietnam. After the first shock, the Americans and their allies fought back and defeated the attacks. Despite the US victory, however, the Tet Offensive confirmed the growing fear that the United States would ultimately lose the war.

Unexpected Resistance

US ground forces had been in Vietnam since spring 1965 to support South Vietnam in its war against its communist neighbor. Many Americans expected an easy victory. But US troops found themselves facing an enemy whose tactics took away the advantages of the modern US Army.

American Opinion

The North Vietnamese government was prepared to suffer huge losses, because it had loyal support from its population. Many Americans, however, were not clear about why US soldiers were losing their lives in a faraway land. As they watched the Tet Offensive on their TV screens, it became clear to many that the United States could not win the war. It was time to find an alternative solution to end the fighting.

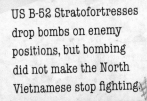

US B-52 Stratofortresses drop bombs on enemy positions, but bombing did not make the North Vietnamese stop fighting.

US tanks are held up behind a farmer's ox cart. The war was mainly fought in the countryside with no fixed front lines.

Vietnam Divided

The modern-day country of Vietnam, in Southeast Asia, was known as Indochina in the 19th century, when it was conquered by the French. The French were eager to exploit Vietnam's natural resources, which included gold, silver, and precious stones, as well as silk, spices, and rice. In 1887, the French made Vietnam a colony of their empire, called French Indochina.

Vietminh troops parade through North Vietnam's capital, Hanoi, in January 1955, after the country became independent.

By the end of the 19th century, up to 50,000 French people lived in Indochina. They treated the local people badly, which led to frequent uprisings against the unpopular rulers.

World War II

When war began in Europe in 1939, Japan took over Indochina. Its rule lasted only until its defeat in the war in 1945. But local communists, led by Ho Chi Minh, did not want the French to resume their control. The Vietnamese were tired of being ruled by foreigners. They backed Ho Chi Minh, who declared himself president of Vietnam in August 1945.

DIEN BIEN PHU

Dien Bien Phu was a French base behind enemy lines in North Vietnam, 10 miles (16 km) from the border with Laos. Some 16,000 French troops were stationed there. On March 20, 1954, the North Vietnamese laid siege to the base. For six weeks, the French were unable to get supplies into the base, while the men there came under constant shelling. On May 7, 1954, the French were forced to surrender. More than 2,200 French troops had died.

In October 1945 French troops returned to Vietnam. They resumed colonial rule of the southern part of the country, but Ho Chi Minh and the communists controlled the north. With the backing of China and the Soviet Union, Ho created a communist state. In January 1946 he became president of the Democratic Republic of Vietnam, or North Vietnam.

The First Indochina War

The south was initially called the Republic of Cochin-China; it later became South Vietnam. The French and the communists both wanted to control the whole country. The First Indochina War broke out between the French and the Vietminh, Ho's nationalist movement, in December 1946.

South Vietnamese leader Ngo Dinh Diem (left) joins French officials as the French surrender Vietnam in September 1954.

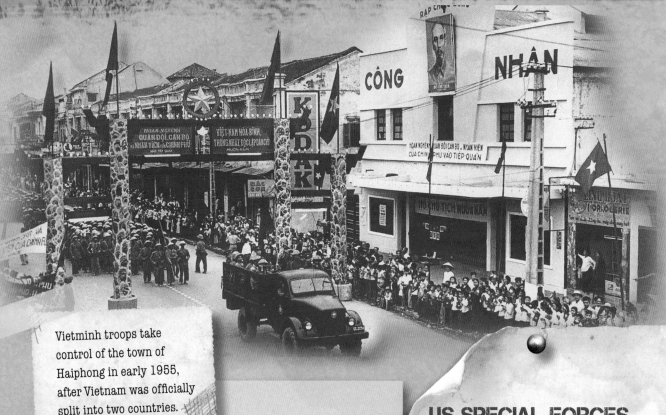

Vietminh troops take control of the town of Haiphong in early 1955, after Vietnam was officially split into two countries.

Defeat for France

After eight years of fighting, the French eventually lost the war. The French army surrendered after a long siege of their base at Dien Bien Phu in 1954. Vietnam was divided officially into the North and the South. The backing of the Soviet Union and China made North Vietnam the stronger country of the two. The US government was worried the communists would take over their southern neighbor. It sent special forces advisors to help the South Vietnamese avoid a possible attack. The first US troops arrived on January 1, 1955.

US SPECIAL FORCES

US involvement in Vietnam started on a small scale when the first US advisors arrived on January 1, 1955. Their brief was to train South Vietnam's armed forces to be able to prevent the country falling to North Vietnam. Green Berets, Navy SEALs, US Rangers, and other special forces were some of the first US units to arrive. The Green Berets were trained in unconventional warfare. They spoke Vietnamese and worked to get the support of local people.

US Arrival in Vietnam

A US Green Beret instructs recruits from one of Vietnam's hill villages at a commando firing range in South Vietnam.

The United States had no intention of fighting a large-scale war in Vietnam. They initially sent advisors to help the Army of South Vietnam (ARVN). Even when regular troops arrived, US commanders still saw their involvement in Southeast Asia as being limited.

After the first special advisors arrived in 1955, the numbers of US personnel in South Vietnam rose steadily. The increased numbers were a response to the worsening situation in the South. Communist sympathizers had launched an insurgency against the government. In 1959, the North invaded the neighboring country of Laos. It sent 300,000 men to build invasion routes leading to the South.

Protecting an Ally

By 1962 there were some 4,000 US military personnel in South Vietnam. The United States wanted to stop the possible spread of communism throughout the region by keeping the South Vietnamese government in power.

US officers patrol with members of the South Vietnamese Army (ARVN); the long antennae are for radio communications.

THE DOMINO THEORY

The "domino theory" was a powerful influence on US policy during the Cold War, when the United States tried to balance the communist Soviet Union's attempts to spread its influence around the globe. The theory argued that, if a country became communist, its neighbor was more likely to follow. The US government believed that if Vietnam fell to the communists, Cambodia and Laos might follow. That would make the whole of Southeast Asia communist—so it was essential to defeat North Vietnam.

US Marines land at Da Nang in South Vietnam in April 1965; US special advisors had already been in the country for years.

A Growing Commitment

In the United States, President John F. Kennedy promised to increase assistance to South Vietnam in 1961 and 1962. After Kennedy was assassinated in November 1963, Vice President Lyndon B. Johnson became president. Meanwhile, in South Vietnam a military coup overthrew the corrupt regime of President Diem. The instability in South Vietnam made Johnson even more determined to support his allies.

Gulf of Tonkin Incident

By the end of 1963, there were 15,000 US military advisors in South Vietnam. Johnson wanted to increase US involvement still further, but was reluctant to do so without the approval

Lyndon B. Johnson greatly increased the US military presence in Vietnam—but still did not want to fight a full-scale war.

LYNDON B. JOHNSON

Lyndon B. Johnson became president in 1963, following the death of John F. Kennedy. During his presidency, he signed into law the Civil Rights Act (1964), the widest-reaching civil rights legislation since the Civil War. Johnson's popularity was undermined by his decision to send more troops to Vietnam, and he became increasingly unpopular. He asked for peace talks with North Vietnam in 1968, but did not stand for reelection that year. Johnson died of a heart attack before the Vietnam War ended.

of voters. His chance came on August 2, 1964, when three North Vietnamese boats attacked the USS *Maddox* in the Gulf of Tonkin, off the North Vietnamese coast. The *Maddox* was attacked again two days later. It fought back, sinking at least one North Vietnamese boat. In response, the US Congress passed the "Gulf of Tonkin Resolution." This gave the president far-reaching powers to wage war as he saw fit in Southeast Asia in order to protect US personnel there. In spring 1965 the first major detachment of US ground troops arrived in South Vietnam.

An Elusive Enemy

A Vietminh antiaircraft unit watches the skies during the war with France. Many Vietminh went on to fight for North Vietnam.

The Americans found themselves facing a different kind of enemy from what they were used to. The North Vietnamese enlisted the whole population in the fight, and also had the support of many sympathizers among the South Vietnamese. These guerrillas were known as the Vietcong.

Ho Chi Minh believed that enlisting the support of Vietnam's peasants was the key to fighting a long war for independence.

HO CHI MINH

Ho Chi Minh ("He Who Enlightens") inspired Vietnam's independence movement. He led the nationalist Vietminh from 1941 and established the communist Democratic Republic of Vietnam (North Vietnam), becoming its president. With his colleague, General Giap, Ho organized the campaign against South Vietnam and the United States before his death in 1969. After the end of the war in 1975, Saigon was renamed Ho Chi Minh City in his honor.

US troops and commanders were trained in conventional warfare. Their tactics were based on fighting battles in large units against similar forces. In Vietnam, this did not happen.

Enemy Tactics

The enemy hid in the jungles and mountains of Vietnam, where US tanks were of limited use. They operated in small groups, launching ambushes on US patrols. When attacked, they simply melted away. The Americans found it difficult to distinguish between enemy fighters and the farmers who lived in the rural villages.

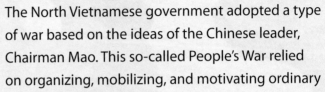

This member of the Vietcong wears ordinary peasant clothes. The Americans found it hard to tell fighters from civilians.

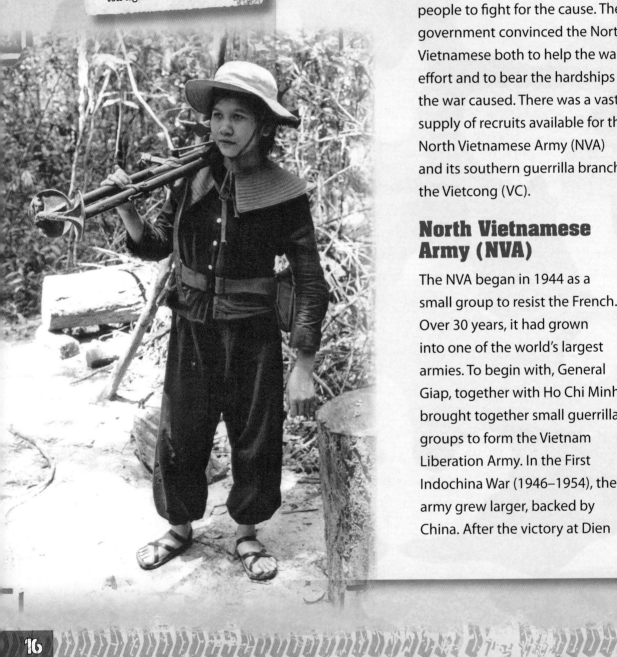

The North Vietnamese government adopted a type of war based on the ideas of the Chinese leader, Chairman Mao. This so-called People's War relied on organizing, mobilizing, and motivating ordinary people to fight for the cause. The government convinced the North Vietnamese both to help the war effort and to bear the hardships the war caused. There was a vast supply of recruits available for the North Vietnamese Army (NVA) and its southern guerrilla branch, the Vietcong (VC).

North Vietnamese Army (NVA)

The NVA began in 1944 as a small group to resist the French. Over 30 years, it had grown into one of the world's largest armies. To begin with, General Giap, together with Ho Chi Minh, brought together small guerrilla groups to form the Vietnam Liberation Army. In the First Indochina War (1946–1954), the army grew larger, backed by China. After the victory at Dien

Members of the Vietcong celebrate the capture of the US armored troop carrier on which they are standing.

Bien Phu in 1954, the army numbered 380,000 soldiers. Recruits were highly trained, disciplined, and well led—unlike their counterparts in the southern army.

The Vietcong

The VC were based in South Vietnam, but their weapons, commanders, and reinforcements came from the NVA. The VC relied on guerrilla tactics, such as ambush, terrorism, and sabotage. The VC usually operated in small units until January 1968, when up to 500,000 VC and NVA fighters combined to launch the Tet Offensive.

REVOLUTIONARY WAR

Ho Chi Minh took his ideas about war from Chinese leader Mao Zedong. Mao believed that a "people's war" should promise a new social order to gain wide support. That support meant a campaign could continue indefinitely. The enemy would be worn down by guerrilla tactics and mobile warfare. Ho knew the Americans did not have the will to fight a long war. By contrast, the Tet Offensive showed that the communists were willing to suffer huge casualties but still keep fighting.

America's Southern Allies

President Diem of South Vietnam (right) meets US President Eisenhower (left) on a visit to Washington, DC, in May 1957.

The United States went to war to prevent South Vietnam from becoming a communist state. To achieve this, the US government relied on the South Vietnamese government. US soldiers had to work closely with their allies in the Army of the Republic of Vietnam (ARVN).

When the United States first became involved in Vietnam, many senior figures at home were concerned. South Vietnam's president, Ngo Dinh Diem, was unpopular and corrupt. But the

Americans also hoped he could provide strong leadership. By the end of the 1950s, however, Diem's unstable government was increasingly reliant on the United States for support.

US Encouraged Coup

Corruption also badly affected the ARVN. When the US ambassador in Saigon, Henry Cabot Lodge, learned of an army plot to overthrow Diem, President Kennedy went on TV on September 2, 1963, and criticized Diem. This was the signal that Washington supported the coup. Diem was overthrown two months later.

SOUTH VIETNAM'S ARMY

The Army of the Republic of Vietnam (ARVN) was originally trained by the French. During the 1960s, it was well equipped and trained—thanks to the United States—and numbered more than a million troops. But the ARVN suffered from poor leadership and corruption, with low-paid soldiers and officers selling equipment to make money. The ARVN suffered from low morale and high rates of desertion throughout the war.

South Vietnamese marines leave a US helicopter during an operation in 1963. That year, the South suffered major defeats.

Westmoreland's Plan

General Westmoreland (in cap) visits a training center for ARVN troops in Saigon in November 1964.

From 1964 to 1968, General William Westmoreland was in charge of all US troops in Vietnam. He believed he needed more men to defeat the North, but President Johnson was determined to fight a "limited" war, with as few US troops as possible.

Westmoreland's strategy had two parts. Ground forces would use "search and destroy" tactics against the enemy, while US aircraft would bomb targets in the North. Westmoreland hoped to wear down the enemy. But with high morale in the North and a constant stream of NVA recruits, his plan could not succeed.

A Failed Strategy

The Tet Offensive of 1968 showed how ineffective Westmoreland's strategy was. US politicians dramatically raised the number of troops sent to Vietnam—but it was too late to make a real difference.

SEARCH AND DESTROY

Westmoreland intended to use huge quantities of US firepower to inflict maximum casualties on the Vietcong and NVA. Infantry patrolled the countryside, either on foot or in helicopters, to locate enemy forces. When they found them, they called in artillery or air strikes to destroy them. The strategy largely failed because US troops were usually responding to VC and NVA initiatives, so the communists set the pace—and were usually able to get away.

US Marines carry out a search-and-destroy mission against the Vietcong near one of South Vietnam's many rural villages.

Battles of 1966–1967

By 1966 Vietnam was America's war, with ten times as many US troops involved than at the start of the war just a year earlier. By the end of 1967, the total was almost half a million. But the enemy continued to fight small clashes using guerrilla tactics.

A US Skyraider drops a phosphorus bomb on a target in February 1966. The chemical causes terrible burns to the skin.

US infantry are evacuated by UH-1 Hueys after a mission in March 1966. Helicopters were the best way to get around.

On January 8, 1966, the Americans launched the biggest offensive of the war to date. In Operation Crimp, almost 8,000 troops were deployed to locate and destroy the Vietcong's headquarters in Saigon, South Vietnam.

Hidden HQ

Despite raining bombs onto the Chu Chi area of Saigon for 42 days, the Americans failed to find the VC headquarters. Later, they discovered that the VC used a vast network of underground tunnels, from which they emerged at night. The tunnels housed the headquarters, as well as living quarters, hospitals, and storage space.

THE HELICOPTER WAR

In Vietnam the helicopter became the most important piece of hardware for the US Army. It was perfectly suited to the Vietnamese terrain: it could land in dense jungle or on mountaintops. The US workhorse was the UH-1 Huey, which was used to transport troops and supplies, and to evacuate wounded troops. In 1968, the AH-1 Cobra—a new helicopter gunship—started service in Vietnam. During the war, US helicopter pilots flew more than 30 million sorties.

In March 1965, the Americans had begun Operation Rolling Thunder. The bombing campaign against the North Vietnamese cities of Hanoi and Haiphong was intended to undermine enemy morale. The operation was supposed to last a few weeks, but the North Vietnamese showed no sign of giving up the struggle. Now Operation Rolling Thunder was increased. It would continue until November 1968.

Operation Cedar Falls

In 1967 NVA soldiers continued to infiltrate into South Vietnam. US forces increased their operations against the communists. In January, US and ARVN forces fought the Vietcong in the Iron Triangle, an area controlled by the VC.

A US Special Forces Group patrols a river in the Mekong Delta, a low-lying area of rivers and swamps.

US Marines cross fields on a search-and-destroy patrol in June 1965. On patrol, they were often in danger of ambush.

The allies destroyed hundreds of enemy bases and many supplies. Most of the VC fighters managed to flee, however.

Under Siege

On April 24, 1967, the NVA attacked the US base at Khe Sanh. The 3rd Marines finally drove the attackers off by May 11. The NVA started to assemble for an even larger attack on the base. Meanwhile, the North Vietnamese were planning a huge offensive in the South in 1968, around the Tet celebrations for the new year.

ON PATROL

With the enemy hiding in the jungle and villages of South Vietnam, US forces sought them out on foot. Foot patrols were dangerous, and soldiers hated them. The enemy often ambushed patrols or set booby traps for them. The VC laid mines and set traps like punji stakes. These sharp lengths of bamboo were hidden in covered pits. If a soldier stepped on one, it went through his foot. The fear of finding a mine or trap caused terror among many US troops.

The Siege of Khe Sanh

The US combat base at Khe Sanh lay close to the Vietnamese border with Laos. As the NVA prepared for a siege, US commanders ordered the base to be held. They wanted to stop the communists using the Ho Chi Minh Trail to smuggle men and goods into South Vietnam. But the communists were already making their final preparations for the Tet Offensive.

Shells explode outside the perimeter of the US Marine base at Khe Sanh. During the siege, the base was shelled almost constantly.

Marines wait to fly out of Khe Sanh. The constant stress of being under siege was exhausting for the defenders of the base.

MARINES UNDER FIRE

By late January 1968, Khe Sanh and its fortified hill positions held 6,053 troops: four Marine infantry battalions and an ARVN Ranger battalion. The base could only be resupplied by air; even water had to be helicoptered in. The besieged men had to endure endless bombing, and enemy fire kept them pinned down in their trenches and bunkers. Fog and smoke from the bombs made it difficult to drop supplies accurately: they often fell where the enemy could get them.

The new NVA attack finally began on January 21, 1968. This time, the Marines at Khe Sanh would be besieged for 77 days.

The Siege Ends

The NVA surrounded the base, which could only be resupplied by helicopter. The Marines suffered artillery and sniper fire from the enemy hidden in the jungle. Meanwhile US aircraft dropped 5,000 bombs a day on NVA positions. The siege ended on April 9, 1968, when two US divisions relieved the base. Two months later policy changed, and Khe Sanh was abandoned.

The Tet Offensive

US Marines shelter in elephant grass as they come under enemy fire near Da Nang at the height of the Tet Offensive.

The turning point of the whole war came on January 30, 1968. On the Vietnamese holiday of Tet, the North Vietnamese launched the biggest military offensive of the war. Although it was defeated, the US victory came at an extremely high price.

The Tet holiday, the Vietnamese New Year, was supposed to mark the start of a three-day ceasefire. Instead, on the morning of January 30, NVA and Vietcong forces attacked around 100 towns and cities in South Vietnam simultaneously. The South Vietnamese and Americans were caught completely off guard.

Fighting in Saigon

The main target of the attacks was the South Vietnamese capital, Saigon. Thirty-five communist battalions attacked political and military targets across the city. The aim was to paralyze the city and then to spark a popular uprising among the citizens, who would bring down the South Vietnamese government.

HOLIDAY CEASEFIRE

Up until 1968, both sides had observed a ceasefire during the three days of Tet. The festival celebrates the Vietnamese New Year and is the biggest holiday of the year. It is a chance for people to return to their family homes to celebrate together. In 1968, radio stations across Vietnam announced the ceasefire—but unknown to the South Vietnamese and the Americans, the North Vietnamese had already celebrated Tet. Now they were ready to attack.

US infantry and M113 armored personnel carriers exchange fire with the enemy in Long Binh during the Tet Offensive.

A member of the US 1st Air Cavalry Division keeps watch during an operation to clear the enemy from a rural area.

The US embassy was attacked by a 19-man Vietcong squad. It failed to penetrate the embassy's tight security. The Vietcong did make some headway, but were stopped by the quick reaction of US troops and the ARVN. The people of Saigon did not rise up against the government.

Fighting Continues

Within 10 days, the Tet Offensive was over. The VC were nearly wiped out. General Westmoreland was relieved by his victory. However, President Johnson refused his request for more troops. At home, the public was shocked. They did not see the Tet Offensive as a great victory. Americans were horrified by the attack on the US embassy, which was broadcast on TV. It was clear that the enemy were prepared to keep fighting, whatever the cost. Many Americans were not prepared to make such sacrifices.

Protest and Response

Across the country, people protested the war in huge numbers. Johnson announced that he would begin to withdraw troops from Vietnam. He also decided not to run in the presidential election in 1968. As Ho Chi Minh had planned, the Americans were losing their will to fight on.

ENEMY DIVERSION

In September 1967 the communists began to attack US garrisons across South Vietnam. General Westmoreland believed the enemy had changed tactics and begun to fight in the open. He also thought the heavy losses would weaken the communists, who lost 90,000 enemy casualties. He was wrong on both counts. The attacks were intended to divert US troops from towns and cities while a VC force of 84,000 prepared for the Tet Offensive.

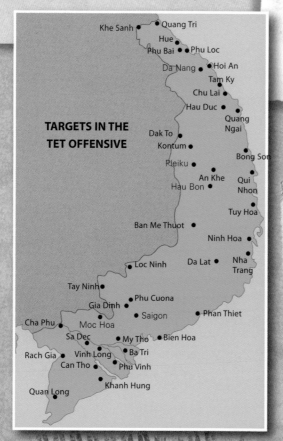

TARGETS IN THE TET OFFENSIVE

Khe Sanh • Quang Tri
Hue •
Phu Bai • • Phu Loc
Da Nang • • Hoi An
Tam Ky
Chu Lai •
Hau Duc •
Quang Ngai
Dak To •
Kontum •
Pleiku •
Bong Son
An Khe • Qui Nhon
Hau Bon •
Tuy Hoa •
Ban Me Thuot •
Ninh Hoa •
Loc Ninh • Da Lat • Nha Trang
Tay Ninh •
Phu Cuona •
Gia Dinh •
Saigon • Phan Thiet
Cha Phu • Moc Hoa
Sa Dec •
My Tho • Bien Hoa
Rach Gia • Vinh Long • Ba Tri
Can Tho • Phu Vinh
Quan Long • Khanh Hung

The Tet Offensive targeted dozens of towns and cities throughout South Vietnam: the attack took place on a massive scale.

THE BATTLE FOR SAIGON

The Tet Offensive targeted dozens of towns and cities across South Vietnam, but the communists' main target was the capital, Saigon. Despite having the element of surprise, they failed to capture the city. US and ARVN forces scrambled to mount an effective defense.

ARVN Special Forces patrol along Nguyen Binh Khien Street in Saigon during the counterattack against the Tet Offensive.

Residents of a Saigon suburb hunt for survivors and belongings in the rubble of their homes after a rocket attack.

THE WAR ON TV

Vietnam was the first conflict beamed directly into US homes. Each night, families watched images of the fighting. TV coverage became more important as more people wondered why the government was fighting what seemed to be an unwinnable war. Images of the storming of the US embassy convinced many Americans that it was time to leave Vietnam. When the veteran TV journalist Walter Cronkite said the same thing on the evening news, many people agreed.

In the early fighting, 19 VC fought a six-hour battle with US military police guarding the US embassy. The VC were eventually killed, but Americans watching the drama live on TV were outraged. They were deeply upset that the VC had penetrated the heart of US power in Vietnam.

End of the Offensive

Across Saigon, VC attacks made early gains. Fighting was very heavy at the Tan Son Nhut airbase, where the VC fought hand-to-hand with US soldiers. The communists suffered heavy losses. It was the same across Saigon, and the offensive collapsed in just a few days.

The Battle for Hue

The imperial city of Hue was the scene of some of the heaviest fighting of the Tet Offensive. Both sides believed a victory in the city would be highly symbolic. The communists hoped that the people of Hue would support them against the US and ARVN. In fact, few people rose up in their support.

Men of the US 5th Marine Regiment catch their breath before advancing through a blown-up wall during the battle for Hue.

The US Marine counterattack against the NVA left the Citadel, the Old City of Hue, in ruins.

On January 31, 1968, almost 8,000 NVA soldiers launched a coordinated, multipronged attack on both sides of the Perfume River. They quickly overran the ancient Citadel and much of the New City. In the old part of the city, only the 1st ARVN Division held out.

Allied Forces

The nearest US troops were 7 miles (11 km) away, although, around 200 US and Australian troops held a compound in the New City. Allied commanders vastly underestimated the numbers of the enemy. They initially sent too few reinforcements: just a single company.

THE CITADEL

The Perfume River divides Hue in two. The Citadel, the ancient walled city, sits on the north bank; the New City is on the south bank. The ancient city saw some of the heaviest fighting. Built in the early 19th century, the Citadel contains the former Imperial Palace, market squares, and pagodas with moats. Its ramparts and high towers gave it the appearance of a medieval walled town. The Citadel was the cultural heart of Vietnam—but the fighting for Hue left it in ruins.

As the scale of the attack became clear, US commanders sent in more troops. They made little initial headway against an enemy that far outnumbered them. The streets were too narrow to use tanks. US Marines went house to house, using hand-to-hand combat to clear the enemy from hiding places among the buildings.

Gradual Victory

The bitter street fighting lasted two weeks. By February 9, 1968, the Marines had cleared most of the New City. Fighting continued in the Old City, however, until the Imperial Palace was finally captured on February 24.

US Marine riflemen use a captured building for shelter as they search for enemy snipers lying in wait for their colleagues.

Marines set up a mortar in Hue. Mortars fire shells in a high arc, so they are used against enemy positions hidden behind obstacles.

URBAN WARFARE

Hue marked a new kind of warfare in Vietnam. There, as in Saigon, fighting took place in narrow streets where US military hardware was useless. Instead, soldiers fought with guns or small arms, or with their bare hands. Every street was fought over until the US 1st and 5th Marines finally recaptured the Imperial Palace on February 24, 1968. Operation Hue City was declared completed on March 2. The death toll stood at 143 Marines and 1,943 communists.

Devastation in Hue

The communists had controlled Hue for nearly a month. In that time, they had killed between 3,000 and 6,000 civilians. Half of the city was destroyed, and 116,000 out of a population of 140,000 were homeless. But in 26 days of intense fighting, the communists had seen their early advantage wiped out as they suffered a stunning defeat. Despite the victory, however, Americans at home protested even more about the war.

Impact on America

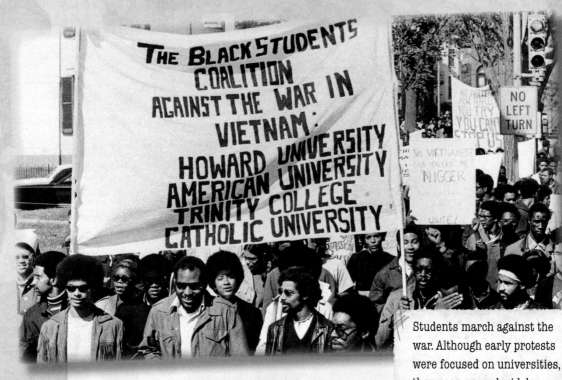

Students march against the war. Although early protests were focused on universities, they soon spread widely through society.

When the war began, few Americans would have been able to locate Vietnam on a map. This faraway country seemed to have little to do with the United States. But fear of communism was a constant threat to the stability of US daily life.

Richard Nixon hits the campaign trail in 1968. He said he would bring US troops home—but was slow to fulfill his promise.

When ground forces went into Vietnam in 1965, protests erupted on college campuses. The protesters were a minority, however. Two-thirds of all Americans backed the war.

Growing Opposition

This changed with the increase in TV broadcasts. By 1967, it was clear that the war was unlikely to be decisive. The Tet Offensive of January 1968 dealt a huge blow to public confidence. Protests became widespread and society became polarized. The war convinced President Johnson to retire and paved the way for Richard Nixon to win the 1968 presidential election.

ELECTION OF NIXON

Republican candidate Richard Nixon ran in the 1968 presidential election on a promise to end the war in Vietnam. It was what most Americans wanted to hear. The Democratic candidate, Vice President Hubert H. Humphrey, was too close to President Johnson to have a chance, especially after the Democratic Party Convention in Chicago in August broke out into riots. Instead, Nixon was elected on a platform of "peace with honor" and "law and order."

From Tet to Defeat

UH-1 Hueys from the US 101st Airborne Division lay a smokescreen to protect infantry operations in the open countryside below.

The Tet Offensive of 1968 was the turning point in the Vietnam War. Despite the allied victory, Americans no longer believed that the war was winnable. Protests across the country persuaded the government that the war had to end.

President Richard M. Nixon had been elected on a promise to end the war. After his inauguration in January 1969, however, US involvement in Vietnam actually increased rather than decreasing. Nixon introduced a new policy of "Vietnamization," which was meant to reduce the number of US troops in Vietnam. However, with no evidence that the North Vietnamese would stop fighting, Nixon ordered the resumption of aerial bombing of North Vietnam.

Illegal Bombing Campaign

Nixon and his chief advisor, Secretary of State Henry Kissinger, also started a secret and illegal bombing campaign in neighboring Cambodia. They wanted to destroy NVA bases there.

VIETNAMIZATION

With public support for the war falling, President Nixon announced in June 1969 that 25,000 US troops would be withdrawn from Vietnam. Reequipped ARVN troops would take over their battlefield duties. He called his new policy "Vietnamization." The South Vietnamese would gradually take more responsibility for the war. This would need more men, so a new law forced South Vietnamese men between 17 and 43 to join the ARVN.

A medic signals for a helicopter on "Hamburger Hill," which US forces captured in May 1969 at a very high cost in casualties.

On October 15, 1969, up to 250,000 people marched on Washington, DC, to protest against the war. Meanwhile US casualties in Vietnam rose to more than 40,000 by the end of the year. The Tet Offensive had undermined support for the war at home. The morale of US troops was at breaking point.

Peace Process

President Nixon announced an organized withdrawal of troops from Vietnam. He also accepted what many Americans had believed since the Tet Offensive had showed that the war could not be won: only a negotiated peace could end the fighting. Nixon sent Henry Kissinger to Paris to meet the North Vietnamese. The North Vietnamese were reluctant to make peace,

US personnel wait to fly home at the end of their tour of duty in 1970; the number of US military in Vietnam was steadily falling.

On April 30, 1975, NVA troops ride through the gates of the Presidential Palace in Saigon. South Vietnam had fallen.

so US pilots launched another bombing campaign against the North. The Paris Peace Accords were finally signed in January 1973.

The Fall of the South

The peace accords guaranteed the survival of South Vietnam—but everyone knew its days were numbered. The communists had no intention of ending the war. When they launched a major offensive in early 1975, the ARVN gave in. The NVA took Saigon on April 30. The war was over. The North had won.

THE BOAT PEOPLE

When the North Vietnamese briefly held Hue in 1968, they killed up to 6,000 people. After South Vietnam fell in April 1975, many South Vietnamese feared for their lives and fled the country. Up to 1.5 million refugees set out to cross the ocean on makeshift boats. Between 50,000 and 200,000 of these "boat people" died from drowning, starvation, or pirate attacks. But many did make it to new homes. The United States accepted 823,000 boat people.

TIMELINE

1945   At the end of World War II, Ho Chi Minh declares Vietnamese independence.

1946   The First Indochina War begins as the French try to reestablish colonial control.

1954   Vietminh fighters defeat 40,000 French troops at Dien Bien Phu. The Geneva Convention divides Vietnam into North and South.

1955   As the French leave Vietnam, the first US advisors arrive to train troops of the Army of the Republic of Vietnam (ARVN).

1957   Communists begin an ongoing insurgency in South Vietnam.

1960   North Vietnam creates the Vietcong to carry out the insurgency in South Vietnam.

1963   With the support of the United States, President Diem is overthrown in South Vietnam.

1964   August: In the Gulf of Tonkin Incident, Vietnamese patrol boats attack US naval vessels.

August: The Gulf of Tonkin Resolution gives President Lyndon B. Johnson power to wage war against North Vietnam.

1965   February: Operation Rolling Thunder begins a bombing campaign against enemy targets in South Vietnam.

April: The first US combat troops arrive in Vietnam.

November: The first major battle of the Vietnam War takes place in the Ia Drang Valley.

1966 Protests against the war grow in the United States.

1967 January: In Operation Cedar Falls, some 30,000 US and ARVN troops set out to clear Vietcong personnel from the Saigon area.

1968 **January: The communists launch the Tet Offensive.**

January: The US Marine base at Khe Sanh is besieged; the siege will last until April.
February: US forces defeat the enemy in the Battle of Hue.

March: President Johnson announces that he will not stand for reelection.

November: Richard M. Nixon is elected US president after promising to end the war.

1969 May: The Americans announce a policy of "Vietnamization."

November: The largest antiwar demonstration yet takes place in Washington, DC.

1970 The United States and North Vietnam resume secret peace talks.

1972 Nixon orders further reductions in US troop levels in Vietnam.

A new bombing campaign is launched against North Vietnam to force it to negotiate at peace talks.

1973 A ceasefire is agreed; the last US troops leave Vietnam.

1975 A major communist offensive sweeps into South Vietnam.

April: Saigon falls to communist troops, and South Vietnam surrenders to the North. Vietnam is reunited under a communist government in Hanoi.

GLOSSARY

ambush A surprise attack made by hidden attackers.

assassination A murder carried out for political reasons.

colony A settlement founded in a territory by people from another country.

communists People who support a society where all property is owned by the state, which in turn supports the welfare of all its citizens.

coup A sudden, violent seizure of power.

guerrilla Someone who fights by irregular means such as ambush, sabotage, and assassination.

infiltrate To secretly mix with a group of people, such as the enemy, without being detected.

insurgency An organized rebellion that uses violence to try to overthrow a government.

morale The fighting spirit of an individual or a group, and how much they believe in victory.

nationalism The wish of a people to govern their own country.

sabotage Destroying equipment and transportation networks to disrupt enemy operations.

siege A military operation in which forces surround an enemy position or town in order to force it to surrender.

special forces Elite military groups trained in unconventional tactics.

strategic Something that is related to an overall conflict, rather than to a short-term victory in a battle.

tactics How commanders arrange and move their forces during a battle.

unconventional warfare Fighting the enemy with ambush, sabotage, and guerrilla tactics, rather than with set battles.

FURTHER INFORMATION

Books

Gitlin, Marty. *U.S. Involvement in Vietnam* (Essential Events). Abdo Publishing Company, 2010.

Kent, Deborah. *The Vietnam War: From Da Nang to Saigon* (The United States at War). Enslow Publishing Inc, 2011.

McNeese, Tim. *The Cold War and Postwar America, 1946–1963*. Chelsea House Publications, 2010.

O'Connell, Kim A. *Primary Source Accounts of the Vietnam War* (America's Wars through Primary Sources). Myreportlinks.com, 2006.

Tougas, Shelley. *Weapons, Gear, and Uniforms of the Vietnam War* (Edge Books). Capstone Press, 2012.

Wiest, Andrew. *The Vietnam War* (Essential Histories: War and Conflict in Modern Times). Rosen Publishing Group, 2008.

Websites

www.pbs.org/wgbh/amex/vietnam/
Online companion to the PBS series *Vietnam: A Television History*.

www.spartacus.schoolnet.co.uk/vietnam.htm
Spartacus Educational page with links to biographies and other articles.

www.history.com/topics/vietnam-war
History.com page of links about the Vietnam War.

Publisher's note to educators and parents: Our editors have carefully reviewed these websites to ensure that they are suitable for students. Many websites change frequently, however, and we cannot guarantee that a site's future contents will continue to meet our high standards of quality and educational value. Be advised that students should be closely supervised whenever they access the Internet.

INDEX